Two
In the Kitchen

A Cookbook With a Maritime Flavour

Janet Bell and Janet Lee

Cookbooks with Culture Series #2

Pottersfield Press
Lawrencetown Beach, Nova Scotia
Canada

Canadian Cataloguing in Publication Data

Bell, Janet.

Two cooks in the kitchen

(Cookbooks with culture series ; 2)

ISBN 0-919001-59-9

1. Cookery, Canadian -- Nova Scotia style. I. Lee,
Janet. II. Title. III. Series

TX715.6.B44 1990   641.59716   C90-097572-5

Published by
Pottersfield Press
Lawrencetown Beach,
RR 2 Porters Lake, Nova Scotia BOJ 2SO

902-827-4517

Pottersfield Press receives block grant publishing support from the
Nova Scotia Department of Tourism and Culture

We dedicate this book to our parents - David and Mamie Lee and Stirling and Barbara Ferguson. I want to especially remember my dad who always said that the key to cooking good food was to keep practising a dish until it tasted the way you liked it. He was referring to Chinese food but it applies to anything you cook.

When you write a book, especially a cookbook, it is not done without the help and encouragement of friends.

Thank you to Charlene Grigg, Lee McMemeny, Nancy Lehre, Vince Marsh, Sue Marsh, Marijke Simons, John Davies, Kevin Davies and Mandy McGunnigle. Without their good humor, enthusiasm, and unerring eye for editing we would still be baking muffins.

Joanne Lamey's kind words and critical analysis were invaluable. Elaine Jeffery was just super in providing those kitchen chats so necessary to start and continue this type of project. Colleen Miller was the answer to our prayers. Thank you so much for leading us through the computer forest. You will never know how much it was appreciated.

A very special thank you to Carol Horner.
Carol - your kind offer to share your computer knowledge and expertise was invaluable.

And last, but not least, we would like to thank our families - John and Trevor for enduring the non-stop cooking; our two Christophers for just being who they are; Alison and Andrew who were unfailing in providing a running commentary, and finally Claire, who proved that writer's block is not the only thing that can cause you to stop writing a cookbook - nine months of morning sickness can do the same thing.

Too many cooks never spoil the broth.

Janet Bell
Janet Lee

Janet and I live on the top of a hill. From this vantage point, not only can we see way out the harbour to the Atlantic Ocean, but it also affords us a fascinating view of Dartmouth and Halifax. Living on a hill gives us a chance to sit back and reflect upon what is happening below us.

We'd like to share with you this distinctive Maritime perspective that reflects a way of life, a sense of history, and a way of cooking that is uniquely Nova Scotian.

BREAKFAST

A HIGHLAND BREAKFAST: One kit of boiled eggs; a second, full of butter; a third, full of cream; an entire cheese made of goat's milk; a large earthen pot, full of honey; the best part of a ham; a cold venison pastry; a bushel of oatmeal, made into thin cakes and bannocks, with a small wheaten loaf in the middle, for the strangers; a stone bottle full of whisky, another of brandy, and a kilderkin of ale... Great justice was done to the collation by the guests.

Tobias Smollett, *Humphrey Clinker*, 1771

RISE AND SHINE DRINK

Makes 2 to 3 servings

Absolutely no time to make breakfast? Then whip out your blender and in minutes you've got a delicious and nourishing meal. Definitely worth waking up to.

1 c	orange juice (fresh or frozen)	250 ml
1 c	pineapple or grapefruit juice	250 ml
1	egg	1
1 tbsp	honey	15 ml

1. Put all ingredients in blender. Mix well at medium speed. Serve immediately.

YOGURT SMOOTHIE

Makes 2 servings

Easy, easy, easy to make. And so creamy and smooth.

1/2 c	plain yogurt	125 ml
1/2 c	orange juice (fresh or frozen)	125 ml
1	banana, medium	1
1/2 c	milk	125 ml
3	ice cubes	3
	honey (to taste)	

1. Put all ingredients in blender and blend for 30 seconds at medium speed. Serve.

BLUEBERRY CORN MUFFINS

Makes 12 muffins

A pleasant surprise to eat. The blueberries and cornmeal combination is scrumptious. Perhaps the blueberries you'll be using will come from Oxford, Nova Scotia. Oxford, about two hours north of Halifax, is known as the "Blueberry Capital of the World".

1/2 c	butter, softened	125 ml
3 tbsp	sugar	45 ml
1	egg, beaten	1
1-1/2 c	milk	375 ml
1 c	flour	250 ml
1 c	cornmeal	250 ml
2 tbsp	baking powder	30 ml
1 c	blueberries (fresh or frozen)	250 ml

1. Blend butter, sugar, egg until creamy.
2. Add milk slowly. Stir.
3. Mix flour, cornmeal, and baking powder in another bowl. Add butter mixture. Stir until mixed. Gently fold in blueberries. Do not overmix.
4. Fill greased muffin tins two-thirds full.
5. Bake in preheated oven at 350⁰F (180⁰C) for 35 to 40 minutes. Muffins are done when they spring back at the centre.

On our street, there's an old Victorian mansion that's now a Bed and Breakfast. Janet spent one summer as their gardener. Since I live across the street we'd spend many an afternoon chatting to all their guests. Our children loved looking at all the different license plates, some from as far away as Texas. Janet's favourite couple were on their honeymoon. They obviously wanted to record every moment because they had a camera that went everywhere with them. Janet loves the thought that her gardens have been immortalized on film somewhere in America.

11

MARINATED FRUIT

Makes 4 servings

A snap to put together. Just use the freshest fruits available. Can be made the night before.

4	apples	4
3	oranges	3
1	grapefruit	1
4 oz	grapes (seedless)	125 g
2 tbsp	honey	30 ml
4 tbsp	water	60 ml
2 tbsp	lemon juice	30 ml

1. Heat honey, lemon juice, and water together at low heat.
2. Peel apples if preferred. Slice thinly. Add to honey syrup to marinate.
3. Peel grapefruit and oranges. Break into sections. Combine, along with grapes, into honey syrup. Stir gently to mix fruit.
4. Chill for at least 1 hour.
5. Garnish with mint. Serve.

AND NOW LET us observe the well-furnished breakfast parlour at Plumstead Episcopi ... The tea consumed was the very best, the coffee the very blackest, the cream the very thickest; there was dry toast and butter toast, muffins and crumpets; hot bread and cold bread, white bread and brown bread, home-made bread and baker's bread, wheaten bread and oaten bread; and if there be other breads than these, they were there; there were eggs in napkins, and crispy bits of bacon under silver covers; and there were little fishes in a little box, and devilled kidneys. . . Over and above this, on a snow-white napkin . . . was a huge ham and a huge sirloin . . . Such was the ordinary fare at Plumstead Episcopi.

Anthony Trollope, *The Warden,* **1855**

Janet and her family went apple picking in the Valley last fall. The Annapolis Valley, about an hour's drive northwest of Dartmouth, has numerous fruit farms that let you pick your own apples. The children thought it was all great fun - even more fun when their father got stuck in an apple tree and had to be rescued by ladder.

Janet picked a basket of crab apples and came up with this recipe for cooking them.

CRAB APPLES ON A STEM

Wash but don't peel or de-stem enough crab apples to make two layers in a large pot. Add enough water to cover all the crab apples. Bring water to a boil. Add enough whole cloves to taste. Also add one cinnamon stick. Simmer till cooked. Let cool. Then add sugar to taste. Janet finds that you use less sugar if you add it after the crab apples are cooled. Serve with yogurt.

CURRANT CREAM SCONES

Makes 18 scones.

A classic. What more can we say? Served with raspberry or strawberry jam, a hot cup of coffee or tea; and voila - breakfast.

2 c	flour	500 ml
3 tbsp	baking powder	45 ml
1/4 c	butter, softened	60 ml
2	eggs	2
1/2 c	half and half cream	125 ml
2 tbsp	sugar	30 ml
1/2 c	currants (or raisins)	125 ml
	cinnamon	

1. Mix together flour and baking powder. Cut in butter with pastry blender until mixture forms coarse crumbs.
2. Beat eggs. Add half and half cream and sugar to eggs in separate bowl. Stir well. Add flour mixture and then currants. Stir with fork until mixture is just moist. Do not overmix.
3. Mixture will form ball. Knead lightly on floured board until dough is smooth.
4. Roll to 3/4" thickness. Cut into diamond shapes. Sprinkle tops with sugar and cinnamon.
5. Place on greased cookie sheet. Bake in preheated oven at 450°F (230°C) for 25 minutes until lightly browned. Serve immediately.

ANNAPOLISA APPLE BREAD

Makes 1 loaf

This delicious breakfast bread is named after the Queen of the Annapolis Valley Apple Blossom Festival that is held each spring in Wolfville, Nova Scotia. The Queen is given the name Annapolisa when she is crowned.

1 c	white flour	250 ml
1 c	whole wheat flour	250 ml
1/2 c	bran cereal	125 ml
1 tsp	baking powder	5 ml
1 tsp	baking soda	5 ml
1/2 c	butter, softened	125 ml
1/2 c	sugar	125 ml
2 tsp	grated orange rind	10 ml
2	eggs	2
1-1/2 c	apple, peeled and grated	375 ml
1/2 c	walnuts, chopped finely (optional)	125 ml

1. Combine all dry ingredients in a small bowl.
2. Cream butter, sugar, and orange rind in a separate bowl until light and fluffy. Beat in eggs one by one.
3. Gently stir in flour mixture and apples until just combined.
4. Pour into greased loaf pan 8"x4"x2-1/2" (20x10x7 cm). Bake in preheated oven at 350°F (180°C) for 60 minutes. Cool. Serve.

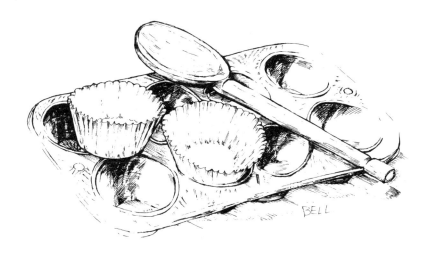

MARMALADE TOASTS

Makes 2 servings

Want a change? Then try our version of French toast. The flavour is wonderful, especially if you use homemade marmalade.

4 slices	whole wheat bread	4 slices
4	eggs, beaten	4
2 tbsp	milk	30 ml
	pepper	
4 tbsp	orange marmalade	60 ml
4 tbsp	vegetable oil	60 ml

1. Spread marmalade on one side of each slice of bread.
2. Whisk eggs, milk together. Add dash of pepper. Pour into shallow pan.
3. Dip bread slices in egg mixture.
4. Heat oil in frying pan on high. Make sure oil is hot. Add bread slices and fry until golden at medium heat.
5. Turn slices of bread over. Cook until golden. Serve hot.

Part of my early morning routine is to check the harbour traffic from my kitchen window. I'm constantly amazed to see the different ships that come into Halifax Harbour, from tugboats to huge container ships and oil rigs. Last year, the most amazing sight occurred. The harbour was completely filled with ice, the first time in over thirty years. The ferries stopped running and people came down to the harbour front to see this sight. Ice breakers were used but to no avail. And so, harbour traffic ceased for close to a week. It was very strange to look out and see nothing but this eerie whiteness. Many of our older friends remember when the harbour actually froze over about sixty years ago and they were able to ride over the ice in horse drawn sleighs to Halifax.

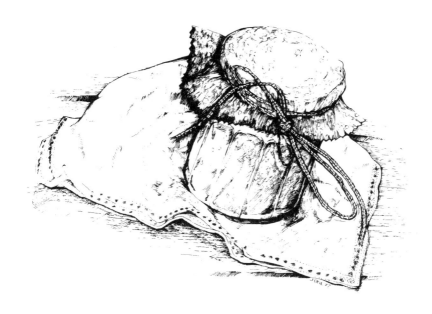

TOMATO AND SWISS TOASTS

Makes 4 servings

A wonderful breakfast. Fabulous for lunch. Makes an excellent hot hors d'oeuvre. Just cut into bite size sections.

4 slices	Swiss cheese	4 slices
2	tomatoes, thinly sliced	2
1	egg, beaten	1
1/2 c	milk	125 ml
	pepper, to taste	
4 slices	bread	4 slices
5 tbsp	butter	75 ml
1 tsp	Pommery or Dijon mustard	5 ml
1/2 tsp	rosemary	2 ml

1. Mix egg, milk, and pepper.
2. Remove crusts from bread. Cut in half. Coat with egg mixture.
3. Melt 5 tablespoons (75 ml) butter in frying pan. Fry both sides of bread until golden brown.
4. Spread mustard thinly on one side of bread.
5. Place cheese slices on top and put on cookie sheet.
6. Arrange sliced tomatoes on top of cheese.
7. Butter each tomato slice and season with pepper and rosemary.
8. Place under broiler until cheese melts and browns. Serve immediately.

BANANA OAT BREAD

Makes 1 loaf

Wondering what to do with those quickly ripening bananas? This loaf is the answer. It's wonderful heated up in the morning for a quick breakfast bite.

1/2 c	butter, softened	125 ml
1/2 c	brown sugar, firmly packed	125 ml
2	eggs	2
1/4 c	milk	60 ml
1 c	ripe bananas, mashed (2 medium sized)	250 ml
1-1/2 c	flour	375 ml
1 tbsp	baking powder	15 ml
1/4 c	rolled oats	60 ml

1. Blend butter and sugar well.
2. Add eggs, milk, flour, baking powder, bananas, and rolled oats. Mix well until batter is smooth.
3. Pour batter into 8"x4-1/2"x3" (20x10x7 cm) loaf pan.
4. Bake in preheated oven at 350ºF (180ºC) for 60 minutes. Cool. Serve.

OATIE ROUNDS

Makes 8 servings

These can be baked in an oven or on a cast iron frying pan on the stove. The frying pan should be lightly floured. Cook only on one side at medium heat as the sides curl if both sides are done.

1/2 c	flour	125 ml
1/2 tsp	baking soda	2 ml
1 c	oatmeal	250 ml
6 tbsp	butter, melted	90 ml
3 tbsp	water	15 ml

1. Mix flour, baking soda, and oatmeal together.
2. Put butter and water in saucepan at low heat until butter melts.
3. Add melted butter to dry ingredients. Mix well.
4. Mixture will form a ball. Knead until smooth. An extra tablespoon (5 ml) of water can be used if mixture does not knead smoothly.
5. Roll out dough on floured board in a round about 8"x10" (20x25 cm) in diameter.
6. Flour a cookie sheet. Put round on it. Bake in preheated oven at 350°F (180°C) for 20 minutes.
7. Cool. Cut in wedges. Serve.

APPLE SAUSAGE BRUNCHIE

Makes 6 servings

Base:

1 lb	pork sausage	500 g
1/2 c	maple syrup	125 ml
1 c	water	250 ml
2 tsp	cinnamon	10 ml
1/4 tsp	nutmeg	1 ml
6	apples (peeled, cored, and sliced)	6

Topping:

2 c	flour	500 ml
1 tbsp	baking powder	15 ml
1	egg	1
1 c	milk	250 ml
3 tbsp	oil	45 ml

1. Brown sausages in skillet. In 9" square (22 cm) pan, arrange sausages in rows until bottom is covered.
2. Bring maple syrup, water, and spices to boil. Let simmer at low heat.
3. Add sliced apples to syrup mix. Cook for about 5 to 7 minutes. Remove apples but keep syrup.
4. Spoon apple slices over sausages.
5. Mix dry ingredients together.
6. Beat egg, milk, and oil together in separate bowl. Add to dry ingredients. Stir until combined.
7. Spoon evenly over apples and sausages.
8. Bake at 400°F (200°C) for 20 to 25 minutes. Top will be golden brown.
9. Reheat syrup. Drizzle over topping. Serve immediately.

The maple syrup run each spring is a Nova Scotia tradition. Many producers hold open house when the sap starts running. It's an experience not to be missed. My little boy, Christopher, is fascinated by the maple sap as it drips into the collector buckets. I love the maple butter and cream, though my favourite is the candy shaped like maple leaves.

GARDEN PUFFY OMELETTE

Makes 2 to 4 servings

This pale, puffed omelette sparked with green is a happy eating experience for 2 to 5 people depending on hunger. It takes just a few more minutes to prepare but is well worth the time.

1 bunch	parsley (or watercress)	1 bunch
6	eggs, separated	6
6 tbsp	water	90 ml
4 tbsp	butter	60 ml
1/2	yellow pepper	1/2
1/2	red pepper	1/2
	dash of tabasco	
	pepper, to taste	

1. Wash parsley. Pat dry. Discard heavy stems. Chop coarsely.
2. Wash red and yellow peppers. Chop coarsely. Saute in 2 tbsp (30 ml) melted butter.
3. Beat egg whites until stiff shiny peaks are formed.
4. Beat egg yolks until thick, then add milk and seasoning.
5. Gently fold 1/4 of egg whites into yolks, then add chopped parsley.
6. Fold in remaining egg whites.
7. Melt remaining butter in large heavy oven-proof frying pan, coating pan with butter.
8. Pour egg mixture into pan and cook gently at low heat until underside is golden and set.
9. Put in preheated oven at 350°F (180°C) until top is cooked, about 1 to 3 minutes.
10. Crease in centre, add yellow and red peppers. Fold. Serve at once.

BAKED BRETON EGGS

Makes 8 servings

These Breton eggs are baked not deep fried. They have a shape all their own. We think the slight lumps and bumps give them character.

8	hard boiled eggs	8
1 lb	pork sausage meat	500 g
1 tsp	sage	5 ml
1 tsp	summer savory	5 ml
	pepper to taste	

Coating:

1/2 c	flour	125 ml
1	egg, beaten	1
1 c	dry, coarse breadcrumbs	250 ml

1. Peel eggs. Eggs must be cold. Put in cold water if necessary.
2. Mix sausage meat with herbs.
3. Dry eggs thoroughly.
4. Divide sausage meat into 8 equal portions.
5. Shape each portion into a round.
6. Completely cover each egg with sausage meat.
7. Roll in flour. Dip in beaten egg.
8. Coat well with breadcrumbs.
9. Bake in preheated oven at 350°F (180°C) in an oiled baking pan for 15 minutes until golden brown. Turn 4 times.
10. Cool eggs before cutting in half. Serve cold.

LADY JULIA'S SALMON SCRAMBLE

Makes 2 to 4 servings

Just an elegant and slightly extravagant way to start the day. The smoked salmon adds a delicate earthy flavour. This also makes a beautiful light supper, served with a garden salad and fresh bread.

4 oz	smoked salmon, chopped coarsely	125 g
4 tbsp	milk	60 ml
4	eggs	4
3 tbsp	butter	45 ml
2 tsp	parsley, chopped finely	10 ml
	pepper, to taste	
4	slices, hot buttered whole wheat toast	4

1. Whisk eggs, milk, parsley, and pepper together.
2. Melt butter in heavy skillet. Add egg mixture and cook at low heat until it sets.
3. Add smoked salmon. Eggs will have a lovely pale yellow colour and should be soft and creamy.
4. Remove from heat and serve over hot buttered toast. Serve immediately.

ONLY DULL PEOPLE are brilliant at breakfast.

Oscar Wilde, *An Ideal Husband*, 1895

During the late 1700s, the Duke of Kent, son of King George II, of England, commanded the British garrison at Halifax. Since there was no residence suitable for a person of his stature, he proceeded to build a country estate on the shores of Bedford Basin for himself and his paramour, Julie, Madame de St. Laurent. Today, all that remains of his once grand estate is the music pavilion, a unique example of a Georgian garden temple.

Janet's friend, Anne, remembers her mother telling stories of summers spent at the music pavilion. Her parents, who lived in Dartmouth, owned it during the late 1800s and used it as their summer home. They travelled there by horse and carriage around Bedford Basin. Anne recalls her mother telling her they used to eat lobsters that had been freshly caught from the waters of the Basin. Nowadays, the only lobsters in the Basin are those in the pounds along the shore which are worth their weight in gold.

TRI-COLOUR PANCAKES

Makes 4 to 6 servings

Zucchini. Zucchini. Zucchini. How do they grow? Try these unique pancakes. Serve with sour cream, fresh fruit, cheese, and bread. They make a real change from the usual breakfast fare.

1 c	zucchini, trimmed and shredded	250 ml
1/2 c	carrot, cleaned, shredded finely	125 ml
1 tbsp	salt	5 ml
1/4 c	onion, chopped finely	60 ml
1 tbsp	butter	15 ml
2	eggs, beaten	2
1/4 c	flour	60 ml
	pepper, to taste	
	oil, for frying	

1. Put shredded zucchini in colander. Sprinkle with salt. Let drain for 30 minutes. Squeeze by hand as much liquid as possible from zucchini.
2. Saute onions in butter at medium heat until soft.
3. Put zucchini, carrots, and onions in large bowl. Add eggs, flour and pepper. Mix.
4. Pour oil into skillet to 1/4" and heat.
5. Drop spoonfuls of batter into oil. Flatten with spatula. Cook on each side until brown.
6. Remove when cooked. Drain on paper towel.
7. Keep warm. Serve immediately.

I NEVER HAD a piece of toast
Particular long and wide,
But fell upon the sanded floor,
And always on the buttered side.

James Paine, *Chambers Journal*, 1884

CAFE AU LAIT

Makes 2 to 3 servings

Ever wonder how to make the French version of morning coffee? Very simple. Very elegant. You'll want a second cup. It's also very nice to have after supper.

1 c	milk	250 ml
2 c	coffee, very strong	500 ml

1. Combine milk and coffee. Bring to a boil in a saucepan.
2. Serve immediately. Individually sweeten to taste.

LUNCH

LUNCHEON . . . is a very necessary meal . . . as a healthy person, with
good exercise, should have a fresh supply of food every four hours. It
should be a light meal; but its solidity must, of course, be, in some degree,
proportionate to the time it is intended to enable you to wait for your
dinner, and the amount of exercise you take in the mean time.

Mrs. Isabella Beeton, *The Book of Household Management,* **1861**

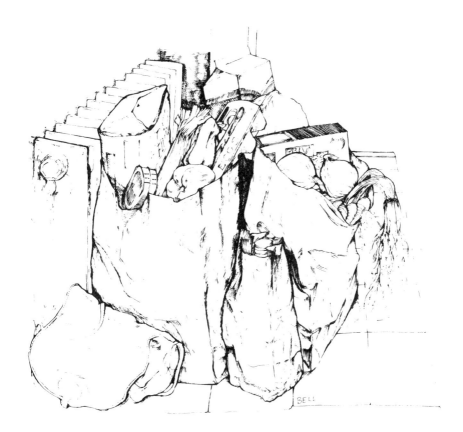

CREAM OF PUMPKIN SOUP

Makes 6 to 8 servings

Howard Dill of Truro, Nova Scotia, has become renowned for his giant pumpkins. He held the World Record in 1979 growing a pumpkin that weighed 438 pounds. All of our children try each summer to grow their pumpkins to this size but alas to no avail. However, their efforts are not wasted as their pumpkins make great soups and jack o'lanterns and perfect heads for "pumpkin people".

4 tbsp	butter	60 ml
1	onion, finely chopped	1
1	garlic clove, finely chopped	1
1/2 tsp	ground ginger	2 ml
1/2 tsp	ground mace	2 ml
2 c	pumpkin puree	500 ml
4 c	chicken broth	1 L
2 c	half and half cream	500 ml
1 c	orange juice	250 ml
	salt, to season	
	pepper, to season	

1. In a large pot, melt butter at medium heat. Add onion. Saute until tender. Add garlic. Saute.
2. Remove pot from heat. Add flour. Stir well. Blend flour with salt, pepper, ginger, and mace. Return pot to medium heat.
3. Add half and half cream. Stir well. Add pumpkin puree and chicken broth. Blend until smooth. Add orange juice. Continue blending. Bring mixture to a boil, stirring constantly.
4. Cover pot. Lower heat and simmer for 30 minutes. Serve immediately.

The joy of living on a hill is all the nice things that are at the bottom. At the bottom of our hill lies Lake Banook. In the Summer, we pack up the children and walk down for a late afternoon swim before supper. There are usually paddlers from the local canoe clubs practising on the water. The children like the war canoes best. When the temperature drops and the lake ice is good and thick we all lace on our skates. Skating outdoors is fabulous. You can skate forever. Located near Lake Banook is the former Starr Manufacturing Company. Two of its former employees invented the spring ice skate. Skates were manufactured there from 1866 until 1938.

CLAM HARBOUR CLAM CHOWDER

Makes 4 to 6 servings

Nothing could be more Nova Scotian than clam chowder. It's got a wonderful taste - not too heavy or rich. Everyone has his own way of making chowder. We hope you like ours.

4 slices	bacon, chopped coarsely	4 slices
1/4 c	onion, chopped coarsely	60 ml
4	potatoes, cooked	4
2 c	clams	500 ml
1/2 c	clam liquid	125 ml
3 c	half and half cream	750 ml
4 tbsp	butter	60 ml
	salt, to season	
	pepper, to season	

1. Fry chopped bacon in a large pot until cooked.
2. Add chopped onions. Cook until soft.
3. Drain clams, reserve 1/2 c (125 ml) clam liquid.
4. Add cubed potatoes, clams, clam liquid, half and half cream, and butter to pot. Mix well. Cook on medium heat for 5 minutes. Stir occasionally. Do not boil. Let simmer at low for 10 to 12 minutes. Serve immediately.

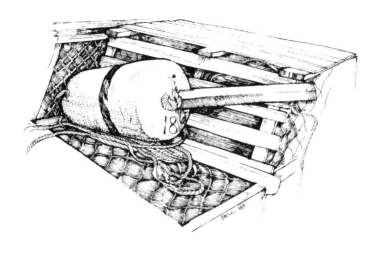

Not only does Clam Harbour have clams but it has a beautiful wide sandy beach and high sand dunes. On a hot summer's day there's nothing like lying on the beach watching the waves and the children making sand castles. It's worth the hour's drive, especially in August when the Annual Sand Sculpting Contest is held. The sculptures have to be completed in five hours, using only materials scavenged from the beach. But you are allowed to bring a shovel.

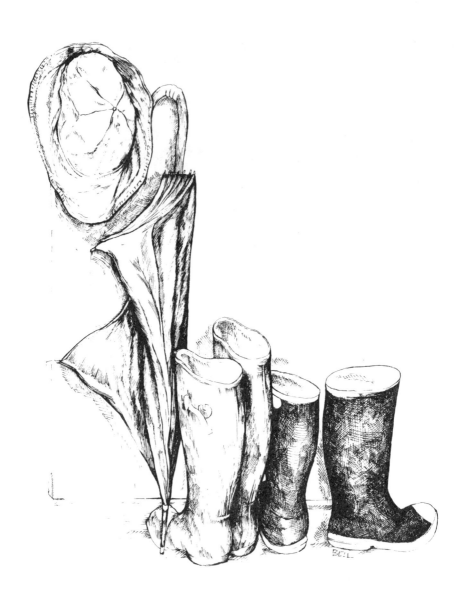

34

MARITIME FISH STEW

Makes 4 servings

Serve this stew on a cold wet rainy night. It will make you feel like you're in the Maritimes for sure.

1 lb	fish fillets (cod or perch)	500 g
2 tbsp	oil	30 ml
1/2 c	onion, finely chopped	125 ml
1/2 tsp	garlic, finely chopped	2 ml
2 c	potatoes, cooked and cubed	500 ml
1	carrot, cooked and chopped	1
1 rib	celery, cleaned and chopped	1 rib
1 c	water	250 ml
1-1/4 c	clam and tomato juice	325 ml
1 can	baby whole clams (10 oz) drained; reserve liquid	1 can
1/4 tsp	thyme	1 ml
	Sherry Pepper, to taste	

1. Heat oil in large pot, add onion and garlic. Cook at medium heat until onion is softened.
2. Add potatoes, carrots, celery, and water.
3. Cut fish into 4 chunks. Add to vegetable mixture along with clam and tomato juice, reserved clam liquid, Sherry Pepper to taste, and thyme.
4. Bring to a boil, reduce heat, cover and simmer until fish is almost opaque in centre, about 10 minutes.
5. Add clams and simmer 2 more minutes until heated through.
6. Before serving, break up fish chunks. Serve immediately.

SAUSAGE STUFFED PEPPERS

Makes 4 servings

Sausage stuffed peppers make a warm, homey lunch. The sausage adds a tasty flavour and is a nice change from the usual ground meat.

4	green peppers	4
1	onion, chopped	1
1	garlic clove, finely minced	1
1 lb	pork sausages, chopped coarsely	500 g
2 c	cooked rice	500 ml
	pepper, to season	
	salt, to season	
1/2 c	breadcrumbs	125 ml
3 tbsp	butter, melted	45 ml
1/2 c	tomato juice or hot water	125 ml
1-1/2 c	tomato sauce	375 ml

1. Wash green peppers. Cut tops off. Remove seeds and pith. Boil in hot water (enough to cover) for 3 minutes. Remove from water. Drain well.
2. In a skillet combine onions, garlic, and sausages. Cook until sausages are done. Add rice and season with pepper and salt.
3. Stuff mixture into peppers.
4. Place stuffed peppers in oiled baking dish. Pour tomato juice or hot water over peppers.
5. Mix breadcrumbs with melted butter. Sprinkle over tops of green peppers.
6. Bake in a preheated oven at 350°F (180°C) for 30 to 40 minutes or until breadcrumbs are brown.
7. Remove green peppers to a serving dish. Keep warm.
8. Add tomato sauce to liquid in pan; heat and pour over stuffed green peppers. Serve immediately.

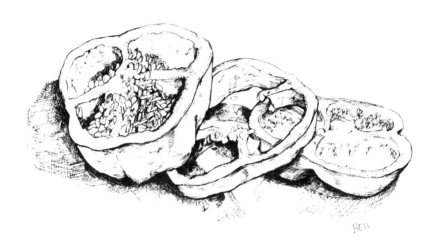

LUNCHEON: as much food as one's hand can hold.

Dr Samuel Johnson, *Dictionary*, 1755

NOVA SCOTIA BEER BREAD

Try this bread! Janet's mom makes this bread all the time. It's so quick and easy. Delicious just straight from the oven, but equally as good the next day if there's any left. Use commercially made beer as homemade beer makes a heavier loaf.

3 c	self-raising flour	750 ml
3 tbsp	sugar	45 ml
1	bottle beer (12 oz)	1

1. Mix flour and sugar together.
2. Add beer. Mix well.
3. Pour into a loaf pan 8"x4"x2-1/2" (20x10x7 cm) and put into a <u>cold</u> oven. Set oven at 350°F (180°C) and bake for 40 to 45 minutes.

BEER STEW

Makes 6 servings

3 lbs	stewing beef	1500 g
1 c	flour	250 ml
6 tbsp	oil	90 ml
8	onions, chopped	8
	summer savory, to taste	
	pepper, to taste	
	salt, to taste	
2 to 3	bottles of beer (12 oz size)	2 to 3

1. Dredge stewing beef in flour.
2. Brown in large pot at medium heat in cooking oil.
3. Add onions to stewing beef. Cook until softened.
4. Add 2 to 3 bottles of beer; enough to cover stewing beef and onions.
5. Simmer for two to three hours. Stir occasionally. If necessary add more beer.
6. Serve immediately.

Maybe it was because of the Army contingents based at the Citadel or the Navy positioned to defend the port, but Halifax has had an amazing number of breweries since it was first settled in 1749. Until a few years ago, Keith's Brewery, located on Lower Water Street, Halifax, was still a working brewery. Founded in 1821, the brewery originally belonged to a Mr. Boggs who sold it to Alexander Keith.

CHEESE SOUFFLE

Makes 4 servings

A souffle is not hard to make. It just gives that impression because it looks so delicate and fragile. The key to making a souffle is to keep a constant vigil on the saucepan while it is on the stove and not to worry.

3 tbsp	butter	45 ml
3 tbsp	flour	45 ml
1 c	milk	250 ml
1/4 tsp	salt	1 ml
1-1/2 c	cheddar cheese, grated	375 ml
4	eggs, separated	4

1. Melt butter in a saucepan at medium heat. Add flour and salt and stir until smooth. Gradually add milk. Stir constantly. Lower heat if necessary. Cook until very thick.
2. Add grated cheddar cheese. Stir until melted. Remove saucepan from heat. Cool slightly.
3. Beat egg yolks well. Add to mixture. Mix well.
4. Beat egg whites until stiff peaks are formed. Peaks should be able to stand. Carefully fold half of beaten egg whites into mixture until just combined. Fold in remaining egg whites.
5. Pour mixture in 1-1/2 quart (1.5 L) oiled baking dish.
6. Cut through mixture all around dish about 1" (2.5 cm) from edge with a spoon.
7. Bake in preheated oven at 350°F (180°C) for 50 to 60 minutes until souffle is puffed and golden brown. Serve immediately.

Sometimes from our hill, we can see the Navy ships come sailing in. Long associated with Nova Scotia, the Navy is a constant and integral part of our economy and history. Seeing these ships, Janet and I have often wondered how you feed all those sailors - especially the quantities needed. Through Janet's husband, we got a recipe for <u>POTATO SALAD FOR 400</u>. Take 120 pounds of potatoes, cooked and diced; 4 pounds of onions, finely diced; 10 pounds of celery, diced; 4 pounds of finely chopped green peppers; 3 quarts of parsley, and 30 pounds of mayonnaise. Combine all the ingredients very carefully a short time before serving. Refrigerate. Makes 400, 5 ounce servings. Honest!!

HAM AND SAUERKRAUT PUFF

Makes 4 servings

Ham and sauerkraut make an interesting combination. The sauerkraut is a tart flavour complement to ham and when baked together in a "puff" - it's an unusual but super tasting lunch.

Puff:

2	eggs	2
3/4 c	milk	175 ml
3/4 c	flour	175 ml

Filling:

1 c	broccoli tops, sliced finely	250 ml
1/2 lb	cooked ham, 1/2" strips	250 ml
1/2 c	sauerkraut; rinsed, drained, and chopped coarsely	125 ml

Vinaigrette:

1/8 c	oil	30 ml
1/8 c	vinegar	30 ml
1	garlic clove, crushed	1
2 c	brick cheese, grated	500 ml

To Make Puff:

1. Combine eggs, milk, and flour. Blend mixture well.
2. Pour batter into an oiled 9" (22 cm) pie plate.
3. Bake in preheated oven at 450°F (230°C) for 15 minutes.
4. Reduce heat to 350°F (180°C). Bake 5 to 10 minutes till light golden brown.

To Make Vinaigrette and Filling:

1. Mix vinegar, oil, and garlic together. Set aside.
2. In a large saucepan cook broccoli at medium heat. Drain well.
3. Add ham and sauerkraut to broccoli. Combine all ingredients.
4. Add vinaigrette. Toss ingredients well. Return saucepan to stove at low heat.
5. Add 1 cup of grated brick cheese. Toss lightly.

Putting It Together:

1. Spoon filling into hot puff. Sprinkle remaining cheese over top.
2. Bake in oven at 350°F (180°C) for 5 minutes until cheese is melted. Serve immediately.

CAULIFLOWER IS NOTHING but cabbage with a college education.

Mark Twain, 1835-1910

LUNENBURG LATKES

Makes 8 to 10 Latkes

Lunenburg, an hour west of Halifax, was first settled by German immigrants in 1753. A beautiful seaside town with streets of heritage homes still standing, Lunenburg evokes a turn of the century feeling. When the fog has rolled in and there's a light mist falling, you can easily imagine what it was like a hundred years ago.

4	large potatoes, peeled	4
1	onion, chopped finely	1
2	eggs, slightly beaten	2
2 tbsp	flour	30 ml
1 tsp	baking powder	5 ml
	salt, to season	
	pepper, to season	
	oil, for frying	

1. Grate potatoes coarsely. Take 2/3 of grated potatoes and wash under cold running water to remove starch. Squeeze out excess water.
2. With remaining 1/3 of grated potatoes, run through a blender or food processor until finely blended.
3. In a large bowl, combine all grated and blended potatoes, onion, eggs, flour, baking powder, salt, and pepper.
4. Heat oil, 1/8" deep in a heavy skillet until very hot.
5. Drop 2 spoonsful of potato mixture into hot oil. Flatten slightly with spoon to form pancakes. Cook for 2 or 3 minutes on either side until golden brown. Serve hot with sour cream or applesauce.

TEA

A TEA TABLE without a big cake in the country in England would look very bare and penurious. The ideal table should include some sort of hot buttered toast or scone, one or two sorts of sandwiches, a plate of small light cakes and our friend the luncheon cake. Add a pot of jam or honey, and plate of brown and white bread and butter - which I implore my readers not to cut too thin - and every eye will sparkle, and all those wishing to follow the fashionable craze of slimming will groan in despair.

Lady Sysonby, *Lady Sysonby's Cookbook*, 1935

TEA SANDWICHES

As our friend Rachel said to us when she first saw our tea sandwiches, "Oh! Good Grief! The bread has no crusts!!" That probably says it all when it comes to making tea sandwiches - trim the crusts. But here are a few more suggestions:

> * Use thinly sliced sandwich bread, either white or whole wheat. Your local bakery should have it. And maybe you'll be able to find pink or green tinted sandwich bread too.
> * Make the sandwiches as close to serving time as possible so they'll be fresh.
> * When the sandwiches have been made, keep them covered with a damp clean tea towel and plastic wrap. Refrigerate them until you're ready to serve them.

TEA SANDWICH FILLINGS

These fillings will bring back a flood of childhood memories of church teas and mother's bridge game lunches.

CLASSIC EGG FILLING

Makes 1 cup (250 ml)

4	eggs (cold, hardboiled, finely chopped)	4
1/4 c	mayonnaise	60 ml
1/2 tsp	curry powder	2 ml

1. Mix all the ingredients together. Use immediately or refrigerate.

Variations:

* Toasted Almond Egg - Stir 1/4 cup (60 ml) finely chopped toasted almonds into Classic Egg Filling just before using.
* Chive Egg Filling - Make Classic Egg Filling but substitute 2 tablespoons (30 ml) fresh chives for curry powder.

MORE FILLING SUGGESTIONS;

* Minced Ham Spread - minced ham, mustard, and mayonnaise together makes a tasty filling.
* Cottage Cheese and Chives
* Cucumber and Cream Cheese - remember to soften cream cheese first.
* Cucumber and Egg - use thinly sliced and peeled cucumber.
* Cucumber and Tomato - use firm tomatoes, they're easier to slice.
* Asparagus and Cream Cheese - fresh asparagus would be nice but canned asparagus is fine. It makes these roll up or pinwheel sandwiches taste just like the ones our mothers made.

BUTTERS FOR TEA SANDWICHES

These butters add a subtle and interesting flavour to any tea sandwich without overpowering the delicate fillings.

Parsley Butter

Makes 1 cup (250 ml)

1/2 c	butter, softened	125 ml
1/2 c	parsley or spinach, finely chopped	125 ml
1/2 tsp	lemon, grated	2 ml
	pepper to taste	

1. Beat all the ingredients together. Make sure they are all well blended. Use immediately, if not refrigerate.

Variations:

* Watercress Butter - substitute 1/2 cup (125 ml) finely chopped watercress. Makes 1 cup (250 ml).
* Watercress Walnut Butter - substitute 1/2 cup (125 ml) finely chopped watercress and 1/4 cup (60 ml) finely chopped walnuts. Makes 1-1/4 cups (310 ml).
* Watercress Cheese Butter - same as watercress walnut butter but substitute 1/4 cup (60 ml) finely grated cheddar cheese. Makes 1-1/4 cup (310 ml).

TEA SANDWICH SHAPES

The dainty shape and appearance of tea sandwiches are very appealing and deceptive. Everyone usually ends up eating more than they thought they did. Here are some suggestions. Remember - trim the crusts.

* Finger
* Triangle
* Double Deckers - alternate wholewheat and white sandwich bread
* Heart Sandwiches - use a heart shaped cookie cutter. Other shapes can be used.
* Pinwheel Sandwiches - use a rolling pin to flatten each slice of bread. Bread should be about half its original thickness. Rolling the bread is the secret to making these sandwiches stay rolled. Spread with filling. Roll up tightly. Slice.

One of the most popular places in Dartmouth, in 1849, was the Tea Garden at Medley's Hotel on Quarrell Street (now Queen Street). At the back of the hotel, there was a large garden with apple trees. Not only did local residents of Dartmouth meet for tea at the Tea Garden, but people would often come over from Halifax.

GOLDEN CRUNCHIE SQUARES

Makes 1 pan

Golden Crunchie Squares are great! They are just like their name -only add the word "sticky". Adults and children alike love them.

1/4 c	butter, melted	60 ml
1/2 c	sugar	125 ml
2	eggs	2
1-1/2 tsp	vanilla	7 ml
1/2 tsp	baking powder	2 ml
1/2 c	wheat germ	125 ml
1/2 c	graham cracker crumbs	125 ml
3/4 c	shredded coconut	185 ml

1. Combine all the dry ingredients together.
2. Add melted butter and eggs. Mix well.
3. Pour mixture into a greased 8" square (20 cm) pan. Bake in preheated oven at 350°F (180°C) for 25 to 30 minutes. Cut into squares while still warm.

CAPE BRETON SHORTBREAD

Makes 1 dozen shortbread

This is a classic shortbread recipe. Buttery and rich, they are a perfect accompaniment to a cup of tea.

1 lb	**butter, softened**	**500 g**
4 c	**flour**	**1000 ml**
1 c	**brown sugar**	**250 ml**

1. Cream brown sugar and butter.
2. Add flour. Blend well.
3. Spread mixture out evenly about 3/4" (2 cm) on a cookie sheet. Prick top thoroughly.
4. Bake in a preheated oven at 300°F (150°C) for 30 to 40 minutes.
5. Cut into squares while still warm.

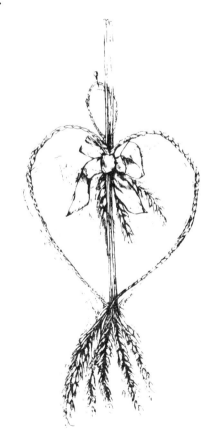

Until just a few years ago, Morse's Tea still did business from their warehouse, down on the Halifax waterfront, as they have for over 75 years. Located in an imposing stone building, Morse's Tea imported tea from around the world. I remember dropping into Morse's Tea a few years ago and leaving with a roughly made teak wood crate from the Orient that still smelled of tea leaves.

LEMON BREAD

Makes 1 loaf

Lemon Bread is the quintessential afternoon bread. It's the mainstay of tea tables from Marion Bridge, Cape Breton to Lower West Pubnico in Yarmouth. This recipe is one my mother has baked for over 30 years.

1/4 c	butter, softened	60 ml
1 c	sugar	250 ml
2	eggs	2
1-1/2 c	flour	375 ml
1 tsp	baking powder	5 ml
1/2 c	milk	125 ml
	juice of 1 lemon	
	rind of 1 lemon	

1. Cream together butter and 1/3 cup (150 ml) of sugar in a mixing bowl. Beat in one egg at a time. Add grated lemon rind.
2. Mix flour and baking powder together. Gently add to creamed butter and sugar mixture 1/3 at a time. Then add half of the milk, another 1/3 of flour, then remaining milk and flour. Be careful not to overmix.
3. Pour batter into buttered loaf pan 9"x5"x3" (12x22x7 cm). Bake in preheated oven at 350ºF (180ºC) for 1 hour.
4. Cool bread slightly. Remove from pan. Loaf should be still warm.
5. Boil together the juice of 1 lemon and 1/2 cup (125 ml) of sugar for 3 minutes.
6. Drizzle lemon syrup over loaf. Cool.

POUND CAKE

Makes 1 loaf

This is a modern pound cake recipe. It doesn't have a pound of butter, a pound of flour or a pound of sugar. But, no fear, this Pound Cake is delicious.

1 c	butter, softened	250 ml
1 c	sugar	250 ml
3	eggs	3
2 tsp	vanilla	10 ml
2-1/2 c	flour	625 ml
2 tsp	baking powder	10 ml
1/2 c	milk	125 ml

1. In a large bowl, cream butter and sugar together. Beat in eggs one at a time. Add vanilla.
2. Mix flour with baking powder. Add flour mixture to creamed butter alternately with milk.
3. Spoon batter into greased loaf pan 9"x5"x3" (12x22x7 cm). Bake in preheated oven at 325°F (160°C) for 1-1/2 hours. Cool.

A LITTLE PEACH in an orchard grew
A little peach of emerald hue;
Warmed by the sun and wet by the dew,
It grew.

Eugene Field, *The Little Peach*, 1889

Years ago, Nova Scotia had a
thriving trade with islands in the
Caribbean. Ships laden with salt
cod would sail from ports like
Lunenburg and Mahone Bay and
return weeks later carrying
molasses and other foodstuffs
which would be destined not only
for Upper Canada but also
Europe. However, not all the
molasses would continue on. It
seems some enterprising Nova
Scotians realized it was one of
the basic ingredients in rum
making. With hundreds of small
coves and inlets, Nova Scotia
provided a perfect haven for rum
runners. Thus was born the new,
albeit illegal, industry of rum
running.

MOLASSES GEMS

Makes 1 pan

Janet's grandmother always had a tin filled with Molasses Gems whenever her grandchildren visited. They have a nice old fashioned molasses flavour.

1/4 c	sugar	60 ml
1 tbsp	butter, softened	15 ml
1/2 tsp	ginger	2 ml
1	egg	1
1/2 c	molasses	125 ml
1/4 c	sour milk with 1/2 tsp baking soda	60 ml
1 c	flour	250 ml
1 tsp	baking powder	15 ml

1. Cream the sugar and butter together in a large bowl.
2. Add ginger, egg, and molasses. Blend well.
3. Add sour milk and flour. Mix.
4. Half fill small muffin tins with mixture. Bake in preheated oven at 400°F (200°C) for 15 minutes or until puffy and brown. Cool.

RASPBERRY SQUARES

Makes 1 pan

My mother makes these squares. Janet's mother makes these squares. Everyone who eats them sighs and reminisces about their mothers making these Raspberry Squares.

Crust:
1 c	flour	250 ml
1 tsp	baking powder	5 ml
1/2 c	butter, softened	125 ml
1	egg, beaten	1
1 tbsp	milk	15 ml
1/2 c	raspberry jam	125 ml

Topping:
1	egg	1
1/4 c	sugar	60 ml
2 tbsp	butter, melted	30 ml
1 tsp	vanilla	5 ml
2 c	shredded coconut	500 ml

Making the Crust:
1. Mix flour and baking powder together. Blend in butter with pastry blender until mixture looks crumbly.
2. Stir in egg and milk. Blend well. Spread over bottom of greased 8" (20 cm) square pan.
3. Spread with jam.

Making the Topping:
1. In a bowl beat egg with fork. Add butter, vanilla, and coconut.
2. Drop by spoonfuls over jam to completely cover. Bake in preheated oven at 350ºF (180ºC) for 45 minutes. Cool. Cut into squares.

Tea can be served plain or with:

* Milk and sugar
* Lemon and honey or sugar
* Sugar cubes soaked in rum
* 2 tablespoons of fresh
  orange juice
* A piece of preserved or
  candied ginger

JUST A CUP OF TEA - FOR 25 PEOPLE

Makes 25 cups

Tea concentrate is one way to make hot tea for a crowd of friends. It can be made ahead of time and the tea tastes as if it was freshly brewed.

| 1 quart | cold water | 1 L |
| 18 | teabags | 18 |

1. Bring cold water to boil. Add teabags to the pot and let brew for 10 minutes.
2. Stir and remove teabags. Pour liquid into a pitcher or teapot.
3. Let stand at room temperature until ready to use but not for any longer than four hours.
4. When ready to serve, pour about 2 tablespoons of concentrate into a cup. Fill cup with boiling water.

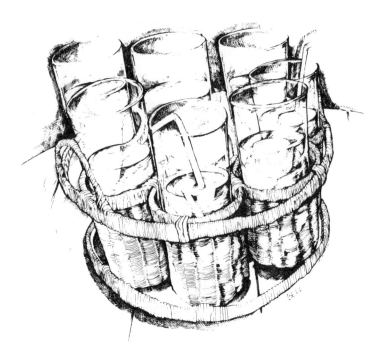

SLIMO

What can we say? Kids are wild about the name and it tastes just as good as it sounds. This is a recipe that Janet's great-grandmother used to make. The number of drinks depends on how much syrup you want to add to each glass. You can buy the tartaric and citric acid at any drugstore.

5	oranges	5
3	lemons	3
2 lbs	sugar	1000 g
2 oz	citric acid	60 g
1 oz	tartaric acid	30 g
2 quarts	boiling water	2 L

1. Grate rind of oranges and lemons.
2. Squeeze the juice from lemons and oranges and add to rind.
3. In a large pot, add sugar, citric and tartaric acid, and juice and rind of lemon and oranges. Add boiling water and stir until sugar is dissolved.
4. Cool. Store in containers in refrigerator.
5. To serve: dilute with cold water (and ice cubes) to taste. Usually about 1/3 syrup and 2/3 water.

HORS D'OEUVRES

WHEN ASKED OUT to dine by a Person of Quality,
Mind and observe the most strict punctuality!
For should you come late, and make dinner wait,
And the victuals get cold, you'll incur, sure as fate,
The Master's displeasure, the Mistress's hate.
And though both may, perhaps,
Be too well-bred to swear,
They'll heartily wish you - I heed not say where.

Richard Harris Barham, *The Ingoldsby Legends*, 1840

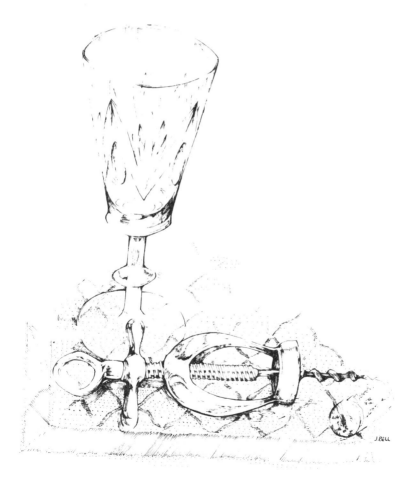

CHEESE DREAMS

Makes 8 to 10 servings

This is a 1950's recipe that Janet's mother would serve to friends after a hand of bridge. It's still popular today with our families and friends. It has a good homey taste to each bite.

2 c	cheddar cheese, grated	500 ml
1/4 c	mayonnaise	60 ml
1	loaf, unsliced white bread	1
1 tsp	Dijon mustard	5 ml
1 tsp	Worcestershire sauce	5 ml

1. Mix grated cheese, mayonnaise, Dijon mustard, and Worcestershire sauce together.
2. Slice bread into 1" (2 cm) slices. Then cut into squares. Remove crusts if you like.
3. Spread cheese mixture about 1/2" (1 cm) thick on bread squares.
4. Bake in preheated oven at 425°F (220°C) until cheese melts and oozes down the sides. Serve hot.

THE HALF-HOUR BEFORE dinner has always been considered as the great ordeal through which the mistress, in giving a dinner-party, will either pass with flying colours, or lose many of her laurels.

Mrs Isabella Beeton, *The Book of Household Management,* 1861

MEXICAN DIP

We know. This recipe has absolutely nothing to do with Nova Scotia. But it is so tasty and so popular with our families that we had to share it with you.

8 oz	cream cheese, softened	250 ml
1/4 tsp	garlic powder	1 ml
1/2 c	sour cream	125 ml
1	large, ripe avocado, mashed	1
1/4 tsp	lemon juice	1 ml
1	large tomato, finely chopped	1
1/2 c	green chilies, finely chopped	125 ml
2	onions, chopped	2
1/4 c	ripe black olives, chopped, well drained	30 ml
1/4 c	green olives, chopped, well drained	30 ml
1 c	tacos sauce, hot or medium	250 ml
1 c	cheddar cheese, grated	250 ml

1. Combine cream cheese, garlic powder, and sour cream. Pour into bottom of an average size serving dish.
2. Add lemon juice to the mashed avocado. Combine with tomato and green chilies. Pour over cheese layer. Spread evenly.
3. Add onions next. Spread evenly.
4. Combine black and green olives. Spread over onions evenly.
5. Pour tacos sauce over olives.
6. Top evenly with cheddar cheese.
7. Refrigerate until ready to serve.
8. Serve with taco or nacho chips.

BELL

CHEESE SPREAD

Feeds 1 crowd

Everyone gravitates to a cheese spread. Little ones love to mush the cheese on their own crackers. At one neighbourhood gathering we had, the adults couldn't get near the cheese spread because of the crowd of wee folk congregated around it.

1 lb	old cheddar cheese, grated	250 ml
1/2 c	butter, softened	125 ml
3 tbsp	sherry	45 ml
	pepper, to taste	
	cayenne, to taste	
1/2 c	walnuts, chopped finely (optional)	125 ml

1. Blend grated cheese with softened butter.
2. Add remaining ingredients and mix well. If too stiff, add more butter.
3. Pack into a crock or small dish. Cover and chill in refrigerator for at least 1 hour.
4. Serve with crackers or toast.

MUSSELS ON THE HALF SHELL

Makes 4 to 6 servings

Until a few years ago, Nova Scotians rarely ate mussels. Instead we were all content to walk past them and leave them lying on the rocks at the beach. Nowadays, mussels are sold right along with clams. With a slightly "sweeter" taste, they are delicious steamed or broiled on the half shell. I think of all the mussels that I have walked by! You can also use oysters or clams instead of mussels.

24	mussels, cleaned and steamed	24
1/2 c	mozzarella cheese, finely shredded	125 ml
2 tbsp	butter, melted	30 ml
1/2 c	bread crumbs	125 ml
	pepper, to taste	
	garlic powder, to taste	
1 tbsp	parsley, minced	15 ml

1. Discard any steamed mussels which have not totally opened. Remove and discard top shells of mussels. Place mussels on a cookie sheet.
2. Top mussels with finely shredded mozzarella cheese and parsley.
3. Mix bread crumbs and melted butter. Sprinkle on top of cheese.
4. Place under preheated broiler for 5 minutes or until cheese melts and bread crumbs brown.
5. Serve immediately.

NAVY PUNCH

Makes enough for 150

2-1/2 quarts	boiling water	2 L
	rinds of 15 lemons finely grated	
	rinds of 15 oranges finely grated	
12 c	sugar	3 L
3 quarts	orange juice	3 L
3 pints	lemon juice	1-1/2 L
9 c	tea, cold and strong	2 L
5 quarts	ginger ale	5 L
5 quarts	grape juice	5 L
4-1/2 gal	cold water	16-1/2 L

1. In a large cauldron, mix sugar and boiling water together. Stir well.
2. Add finely grated lemon and orange rinds. Boil mixture for 10 minutes at medium heat. Let cool.
3. Add lemon and orange juice. Mix thoroughly.
4. Then add tea, ginger ale, grape juice, and cold water. Stir well. Add ice.

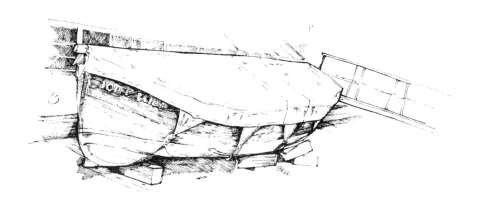

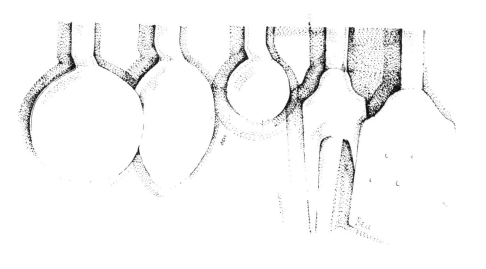

DINNER

LET THE NUMBER of guests not exceed twelve . . . so chosen that their occupations are varied, their tastes similar . . . the dining room brilliantly lighted, the cloth white, the temperature between 60° and 68°; the men witty and not pedantic, the women amiable and not too coquettish; the dishes exquisite but few, the wines vintage . . . the eating unhurried, the dinner being the final business of the day . . . the coffee hot . . . the tea not too strong, the toast artistically buttered . . . the signal to leave not before eleven and everyone in bed at midnight.

Jean-Anthelme Brillat-Savarin,
La Physiologie du gout, 1825

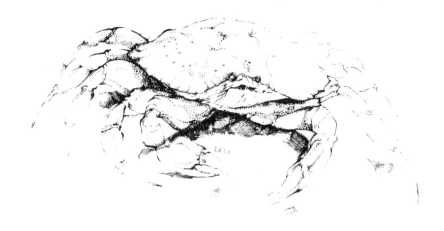

SHE-CRAB SOUP

Makes 4 servings

A dream of a soup - rich, filling, and slightly decadent. The origins of the name are somewhat of a mystery. But Janet and I suspect it refers to the female crab because she carries the roe; and originally the roe was used in making the base.

4 tbsp	butter	60 ml
6 tbsp	flour	90 ml
4 c	milk	1 L
1 tin	crab paste (lobster paste optional)	1 tin
1 tin	crabmeat, drained (6 oz)	1 tin
	Sherry Pepper, to taste	

1. Pour milk into saucepan. Cook at low heat until it begins to boil. Set aside.
2. Melt butter in another saucepan at moderate heat. Add flour and stir until butter and flour are thick and bubbling.
3. Add crab paste to mixture. Blend well. Remove saucepan from stove.
4. Add hot milk to mixture. Whisk often as mixture becomes smooth. Return saucepan to stove. Whisk at moderate heat until sauce thickens. Remove saucepan from stove. Whisk until mixture stops bubbling.
5. Drain crabmeat well. Add to sauce.
6. Flavour to taste with Sherry Pepper.
7. Serve immediately.

SHERRY PEPPER

Makes 1 bottle

You don't need to use an expensive sherry to make this. Pour out about a half a cup of sherry (drink it if you'd like) and add the herbs. It's so simple to make and is a wonderful addition to any soup or even salad dressings. It adds zip and zest. Sherry Pepper makes an excellent gift to give to friends who like to cook.

1 bottle	sherry (1 litre)	1 bottle
1/2 tsp	marjoram	2 ml
1/2 tsp	thyme	2 ml
1/2 tsp	oregano	2 ml
1/2 tsp	fine herbs	2 ml
1/2 tsp	sweet basil	2 ml
1	bayleaf	1
1	garlic clove, peeled	1
	pinch of cayenne	

1. Pour out 1/2 cup (250 ml) of sherry. Add all the herbs to bottle. Shake well.
2. Let stand for a few days; preferably a week.

PEPPER IS SMALL in quantity and great in virtue.

Plato, *Laws*, 360 B.C.

HOMEMADE CRACKERS

Makes 18 crackers

Homemade crackers are a snap to make. Make them once and you'll wonder why you never made them before, they're that simple. These crackers have a light tang to them.

1 c	flour	250 ml
2 tsp	pepper	30 ml
2 tsp	lemon rind, grated finely	30 ml
1/2 c	butter, cold	125 ml
3 tbsp	milk	45 ml
3 tbsp	lemon juice	45 ml
	salt, to sprinkle	

1. Mix flour, black pepper, and lemon rind together. Add to cold butter using a pastry blender.
2. Add milk and lemon juice. Stir mixture until it forms a dough.
3. Roll dough out on floured board until 1/4" (.5 cm) thick. Use 2" (5 cm) round cutter to cut crackers.
4. Sprinkle with salt. Bake on greased cookie sheet in a preheated oven at 400°F (200°C) for 10 minutes or golden brown.
5. Let cool. Serve.

TO EAT IS a necessity; but to eat intelligently is an art.

La Rochefoucauld, *Maxims*, 1665

Yea!! It's summer. Perfect time for a <u>CLAMBAKE NOVA SCOTIA STYLE</u>. For 25 people you'll need 70 lbs (34 kg) of seaweed, 17 dozen mussels, 12 dozen clams, 25 lobsters about 1-1/4 lbs (625 g) each, and 25 medium sized potatoes. Then you need to dig a pit at least 3 ft (1 m) wide and 3 ft (1 m) deep. Preferably do this at a beach but a backyard will do just fine. Line with brick or flat rocks and build a wood fire in it. The fire should burn for about 3 hours so keep adding wood if necessary. You want the bricks or rocks to be white hot in order to cook the seafood. The fire should burn down leaving only coals and ashes. Remove all the coals and ashes after 3 hours. Do this as quickly as possible so the rocks or bricks stay hot. Then lay down a thick wet layer of seaweed on top of the hot rocks or bricks. Now place on top of it the potatoes, then a layer of wet seaweed and then the lobsters, clams, and mussels, separated by more layers of wet seaweed. Cover the top with a final thick layer of wet seaweed. Put a tarpaulin on top weighted down with rocks and then sit back and let it steam cook for about 2-1/2 to 3 hours. The lobsters are done when red in colour and the clams and mussels are done when they open. Discard any that are closed tight. Potatoes are ready when you can put a fork through them. Serve with salad, garlic bread, and lots of lemon slices and melted butter.

SEASIDE MARINADE

Makes 4 to 6 servings

Seaside marinade is a unique way to prepare and serve shrimp, lobster or scallops. If you add a French stick, cheese, and a garden salad - you have the makings of a feast.

1 tsp	salt	5 ml
1/2 tsp	sugar	2 ml
2	garlic cloves, crushed	2
1/4 c	red wine vinegar	60 ml
3/4 c	olive oil	185 ml
2 tbsp	mustard, dry	30 ml
2 tbsp	chili sauce or hot sauce	30 ml
3 tbsp	horseradish	45 ml
1/4 c	parsley, finely chopped	60 ml
1/4 c	onions or chives, finely chopped	60 ml
1 lb	shrimp, cooked and shelled, cooled	500 g
1/4 lb	lobster meat, cooked and cooled	125 g
1/4 lb	scallops, cooked and cooled	125 g

1. In a jar, combine salt, sugar, garlic, and vinegar. Shake well. Add olive oil. Shake.
2. Add mustard, chili or hot sauce, and horseradish. Shake well.
3. Add parsley and onions or chives. Shake well.
4. Combine shrimp, lobster meat, and scallops in a bowl. Pour marinade over it.
5. Marinate covered in refrigerator overnight. Turn occasionally. Serve cold.

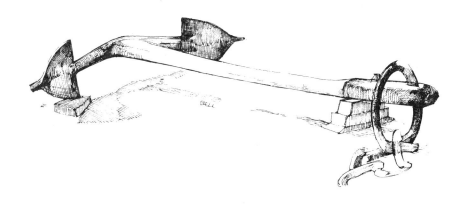

ACADIAN FRENCH STICK

Makes 2 long sticks

Have you always wanted to make bread but were afraid to try? Then you should read this recipe. Acadian French Stick is no knead, no trouble, and very, very good.

1/2 c	milk, scalded	125 ml
1 c	water, boiling	250 ml
3 tbsp	yeast	45 ml
1/4 c	water, lukewarm	60 ml
2 tbsp	oil	30 ml
1 tbsp	sugar	15 ml
4 c	flour	1000 ml
2 tbsp	salt	30 ml
4 tbsp	sugar	60 ml

1. Mix milk and boiling water together. Let cool.
2. Mix yeast and lukewarm water together. Make sure that all the yeast is dissolved. Let sit for 10 minutes.
3. When milk mixture has cooled, add yeast. Add oil and sugar to mixture.
4. Mix flour, sugar, and salt in a large bowl. Pour liquid in all at once. Stir thoroughly to make a soft dough. Pat into a ball. Cover and let rise until it doubles, about 1-1/2 hours to 2 hours.
5. When doubled in volume, punch dough down. Divide in two and form into 2 long sticks.
6. Put on a greased cookie sheet and let rise again until not quite double - about 1-1/2 to 2 hours.
7. Place bread in preheated oven at 400°F (200°C) and bake for 15 minutes, then reduce heat to 350°F (180°C) and continue baking for 30 minutes or until the bread sounds hollow when tapped on the bottom. Cool and serve.

Janet went to the Fortress of Louisburg in Cape Breton for the first time this year. She feels the same way I do about Louisbourg, absolutely amazed and overwhelmed by the sense of history it evokes. Fortress Louisbourg recreates in exacting detail the everyday life of the fort and its inhabitants in the summer of 1744. My parents went there one summer and my mother bought a round loaf of bread from the baker's little boy that had just come out of the huge wood fired ovens. Because the bread loaf was bigger than her purse - she asked if there were bags. The little baker's boy looked at her and very ingenuously said, "I'm sorry, Madame, but there are no bags in 1744". My Mother carried the loaf under her arm for the rest of the day.

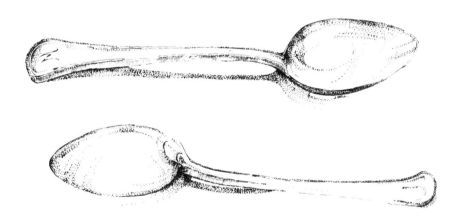

APPLE AND CHICKEN

Makes 4 servings

This apple and chicken dish is one of those recipes that you can prepare and forget about until it is cooked and ready to serve. The combination of apple and chicken is a refreshing change from the usual chicken recipes.

4	boned chicken breasts	4
	oil to brown	
1 c	apple sauce	250 ml
1/2 c	mushrooms, sliced thinly	125 ml

1. In a frying pan, add enough oil to brown chicken breasts lightly on both sides.
2. Remove from frying pan and place chicken breasts in a casserole dish.
3. Pour apple sauce evenly over chicken breasts. Cover. Cook in preheated oven at 350°F (180°C) for 45 minutes.
4. Add sliced mushrooms. Cook, covered, for another 15 minutes.
5. Serve immediately.

DINNER WAS MADE for eatin' not for talkin'

William Thackeray, *Fashionable Fax and Polite Annygoats*

FISHERMAN'S PIE

Makes 4 servings

Don't let the name mislead you. There is no crust to make. Simple and elegant, it is our version of Shepherd's pie.

2 lb	white fish fillets	1 kg
	pepper, to taste	
4	medium potatoes	4
4 tbsp	butter	60 ml
6 tbsp	flour	90 ml
2 tsp	dry mustard	10 ml
2 c	milk	500 ml
1 c	cheddar cheese, finely grated	250 ml

1. Place fish in bottom of buttered casserole dish. Season with pepper.
2. Peel and wash potatoes. Cut into thin, narrow sticks. In a saucepan, cook potato sticks until just tender, about 5 minutes. When cooked, drain water and set aside.
3. In a saucepan melt butter at medium heat. Add flour. Whisk well. Add dry mustard and then gradually add milk. Whisk briskly. Continue stirring until sauce is thick and comes to a boil. Pour sauce over fish.
4. Evenly spread potato sticks over sauce. Sprinkle grated cheddar cheese over potato sticks.
5. Bake for 30 minutes in preheated oven at 375°F (190°C). Serve immediately.

PEPPER FISH STEAKS

Makes 2 servings

2	**halibut steaks**	**2**
2 tbsp	**peppercorns**	**30 ml**
1/4 c	**flour**	**60 ml**
	white wine	
	oil, for cooking	

1. Clean halibut steaks. Pat dry.
2. Crush peppercorns coarsely in a plastic bag. Mix with flour.
3. Flour halibut steaks on both sides.
4. Heat frying pan. Add enough oil to cover bottom. Cook halibut steaks carefully. Turn once.
5. When halibut steaks are just cooked, remove from pan. Keep warm. Add white wine to pan and boil down juices until there is about 1/2 c (125 ml) of liquid left. Season to taste.
6. Place halibut steaks on plate. Pour sauce over them. Serve immediately with rice or potatoes.

FISH IS HELD out to be one of the great luxuries of the table and not only necessary but even indispensable at all dinners where there is any preference to excellence or fashion.

Mrs. Isabella Beaton, *The Book of Household Management*, 1880

DIGBY SCALLOPS

Makes 4 servings

Scallops are bivalves. Our children love the word "bivalves" which means having two valves or halves. It is this action of opening and closing their two halves and squirting water in and out that makes the scallops move quickly through the water. Digby, Nova Scotia, has one of the largest scallop fleets in the world.

1 lb	scallops	500 g
4 tbsp	butter	60 ml
	pepper, to taste	
4 tbsp	onion, minced	60 ml
4 tbsp	lemon juice or white wine	60 ml

1. Clean and wash scallops. Cut larger scallops in half.
2. In a large skillet, melt butter. Add onion. Brown lightly. Season with pepper.
3. Add scallops. Cook and turn for about 5 minutes or until lightly browned. Pour lemon juice or white wine over scallops just before removing from pan. Serve immediately.

AFTER A GOOD dinner, one can forgive anybody, even one's own relatives.

Oscar Wilde, *A Woman of No Importance*, 1894

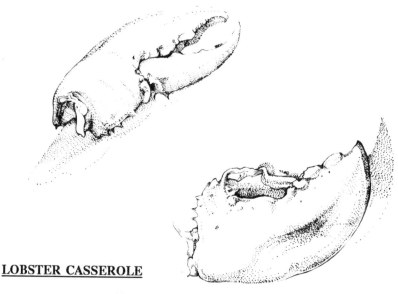

LOBSTER CASSEROLE

Makes 4 to 6 servings

This casserole is easy to make and serve. It's perfect for guests or for a special family meal. If fresh lobster meat isn't available substitute frozen or canned.

2 c	cooked lobster meat	500 ml
4 tbsp	butter	60 ml
1/2 c	mushrooms, sliced	125 ml
1/2 c	sherry	125 ml
1/4 tsp	paprika	1 ml
2	egg yolks	2
2 c	half and half cream	500 ml
1 c	bread crumbs	250 ml
4 tbsp	butter, melted	60 ml

1. In a large saucepan, melt butter at low heat and cook mushrooms until tender.
2. Add lobster meat. Add sherry and paprika. Cook at medium heat for 2 minutes.
3. Sprinkle flour over top. Mix thoroughly.
4. Beat egg yolks and half and half cream together. Add slowly to lobster mixture. Stir until mixture is smooth.
5. Pour mixture into casserole dish. Mix bread crumbs and butter together. Sprinkle bread crumbs over lobster mixture.
6. Bake in preheated oven at 425°F (220°C) for 10 minutes or until top is golden brown. Serve hot with rice or noodles.

NOVA SCOTIA BOILED LOBSTER

Makes 2 servings

It's hard to believe that years ago lobster was considered to be "poor man's meat". Nowadays, lobsters are a real delicacy and their price per pound puts them in the luxury category. But lobsters are well worth the price and effort. Lobster shears are helpful when cracking the shell and so are nut crackers.

2	live lobsters, 1-1/4 lb each	2
6 quarts	boiling water	6 L
1/2 c	melted butter	125 ml
	lemon wedges	

1. Generally lobsters come with banded claws. If they are not banded, carefully plunge lobsters, head first, with tongs, into boiling water. Cover pot, bring water back to boiling. Simmer 15 to 20 minutes. Lobsters should be bright red.
2. Remove lobsters. Drain. Place lobster on its back. Cut lobster lengthwise in half. Remove intestinal vein that runs from stomach to tail.
3. Leave liver (green) or tomally and roe (coral). Lobster lovers consider them to be the best part of the lobster.
4. Serve immediately with lots of melted butter and lemon wedges.

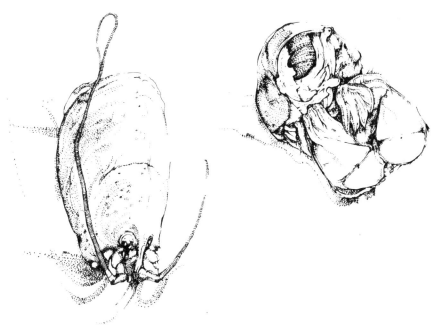

LOBSTER STEW

Makes 6 servings

A tasty, spicy way to eat lobster. You can substitute shrimp or crabmeat.
A quick supper dish, it goes well with a fresh salad and bread.

1/2 c	oil	125 ml
1	onion, chopped	1
2 lbs	tomatoes	1 kg
4	cloves garlic, minced	4
3	bay leaves	3
2 tsp	oregano	10 ml
	salt, to taste	
	pepper, to taste	
2 c	dry, red or white wine	500 ml
2 lbs	lobster meat, fresh cooked, frozen	1 kg
	or canned	

1. Heat oil in large pot. Add onions, tomatoes, and garlic.
2. Cook for 15 minutes at low heat.
3. Add oregano, bay leaves, salt, pepper, and wine.
4. Continue cooking at low heat until wine has evaporated.
5. Add lobster meat. Toss. Serve with noodles or rice.

FRENCH SHORE TOURTIERE

Makes 4 to 6 servings

Between Yarmouth and Digby, in the west part of Nova Scotia, lies the French Shore. Steeped in history and tradition, it has the largest Acadian population in Nova Scotia. When Janet and her family visited there, she marvelled at the easy facility of the Acadians to speak French and English within the same sentence.

	pastry for 9" (23 cm) pie	
1 lb	ground pork	1/2 kg
1 lb	ground veal	1/2 kg
2	garlic cloves, finely chopped	2
2	small onions, finely chopped	2
1/4 tsp	pepper	1 ml
1/4 tsp	thyme	1 ml
1/4 tsp	savory	1 ml
1/4 tsp	cloves	1 ml
1 c	water	250 ml

1. In a large skillet, brown pork and veal. Drain off fat. Add onions.
2. Add the remaining ingredients. Stir. Let simmer until all liquid is evaporated, about 10 to 15 minutes.
3. Add more seasonings if necessary.
4. Pour meat mixture into pastry lined pie plate. Cover with top crust. Seal and flute edges. Make steam cuts in top.
5. Bake in preheated oven at 425°F (220°C) for 30 minutes or until top is golden brown. Serve immediately.

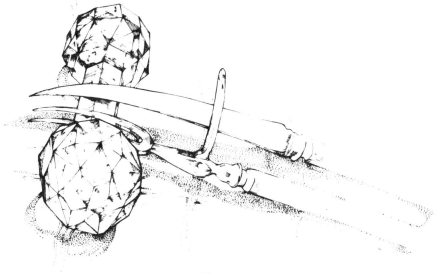

Janet and I are used to living at the top of the hill. Each of us has "fond" memories of pushing a stroller and small child to the top. Each year we know we're in shape when we can finally reach the top - children in tow - without huffing and puffing.

It's absolutely fascinating for us to watch the guests from the Bed and Breakfast returning from an early evening stroll or ferry ride. Those who aren't out of breath when they reach the top, we consider as "honourary neighbours" of the street.

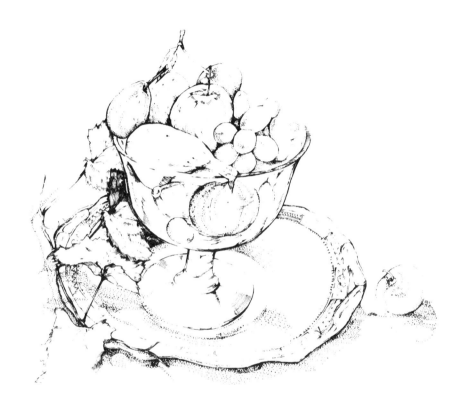

DESSERT

THE DESSERT IS said to be to the dinner what the madrigal is to literature - it is the light poetry of the kitchen.

George Ellwanger, *Pleasures of the Table*, 1903

CLASSIC APPLE CRUMBLE

Makes 4 to 6 servings

Fall in Nova Scotia would not be fall without having apple crumble for dessert. I like to use Gravenstein apples. They have just the right tartness to them to remind you of their freshness and of apple blossoms and spring. An excursion to Annapolis Valley for your Halloween pumpkin always includes a basket of apples.

1 c	flour	250 ml
1 tsp	cinnamon	5 ml
3/4 c	brown sugar, packed firmly	185 ml
1/2 c	butter, softened	125 ml
1/2 c	oatmeal	125 ml
6	medium apples, peeled, cored and sliced	6

1. Mix flour and cinnamon together in a bowl. Add brown sugar and cut in butter. Mixture should be crumbly looking. Add oatmeal to mixture.
2. In a buttered 1-1/2 qt (1.5 L) casserole, sprinkle 1/3 of crumble mix on bottom.
3. Spread sliced apples over crumble mixture. Top with remaining crumble mixture.
4. Cover casserole and bake in preheated oven at 350°F (180°C) for 20 minutes. Remove cover and bake for 30 minutes until top is golden brown.
5. Serve immediately with ice cream or whipped cream.

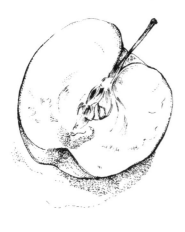

BERRY SHORTCAKE

Makes 8 servings

There's nothing more heavenly than a fresh berry shortcake for dessert. All of us anxiously wait for strawberry season to come. And then we're into a frenzy of strawberry cooking. Of course, then there are blueberries, raspberries, and blackberries. Janet and her little girl had a very successful blackberry picking expedition on the Dartmouth Commons this year. However, after seeing them on their return, I'm not sure if they won or the blackberry bushes did. There's something about blackberry juice smeared all over one's face and clothes that gives berry pickers the look of adventurers.

2 c	cake flour	500 ml
1-1/2 tsp	baking powder	7 ml
1/2 tsp	cream of tartar	2 ml
4 tbsp	butter, cold	60 ml
1	egg, beaten	1
1/3 c	milk	75 ml
1 box	strawberries, or any other berry	1

1. Sift all dry ingredients in a bowl. Cut butter into flour until mixture looks crumbly.
2. Add beaten egg and milk. Mix. Put dough on a floured board.
3. Knead 8 times. Using a rolling pin, quickly roll into a rectangle about 3/4" (2 cm) thick.
4. Cut into 8 squares and place on a buttered baking sheet.
5. Bake in preheated oven at 425°F (220°C) for 15 minutes. Cool slightly. Cut cakes in half.
6. Use whatever fresh berries are in season. Top with whipped cream or ice cream.

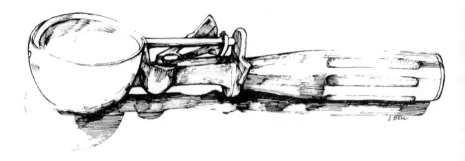

GINGERBREAD

Makes 10 to 12 servings

Hot gingerbread. Ice cream. Whipped cream. It makes me think of Peggy's Cove. In the late fall, after all the summer visitors have left, we like to go out to Peggy's Cove and sit on the rocks and look at the Atlantic Ocean. Even after countless visits, it still is fascinating to drive past all the strange and mystical rock formations created thousands of years ago by melting glaciers. There is a cafe we always stop at on the way back that serves piping hot gingerbread and tea. Nothing warms you up quicker.

1-1/2 c	flour	375 ml
1-1/2 tsp	baking soda	7 ml
1-1/2 tsp	ginger	7 ml
1 tsp	cinnamon	5 ml
1	egg, beaten	1
1/4 c	sugar	60 ml
1/2 c	molasses	125 ml
1/2 c	boiling water	125 ml
1/2 c	oil	125 ml

1. Combine all dry ingredients in a large bowl. Add eggs, sugar and molasses. Mix well.
2. Add boiling water and oil. Mix thoroughly, until smooth.
3. Pour into a buttered and floured 9 inch (22 cm) square cake pan.
4. Bake in preheated oven at 350°F (180°C) for 30 to 35 minutes. Serve warm.

FROZEN RHUBARB FOOL

Makes 6 to 8 servings

Janet's rhubarb grew 3 feet high this year. It was so bushy and thick. The rhubarb was a gorgeous reddish green colour. I told Janet that her rhubarb was so prolific and lush that I was going to tell everyone that baby Claire was found under her rhubarb and not in a cabbage patch.

| 1 c | whipping cream | 250 ml |
| 2 c | rhubarb, stewed and sweetened | 500 ml |

1. Whip cream until stiff.
2. Fold rhubarb into whipped cream.
3. Pour mixture into an 9 inch (22x4 cm) pie plate and freeze.
4. Remove from freezer 20 minutes before serving.

LEMON SYLLABUB

Makes 4 to 6 servings

Refreshingly simple to make but so elegant.

1/2 c	white wine, dry	125 ml
4 tbsp	lemon juice	60 ml
4 tsp	lemon rind, finely grated	20 ml
1/2 c	sugar	125 ml
1-1/4 c	whipping cream	310 ml

1. Mix white wine, lemon juice, lemon rind, and sugar together in a bowl. Cover and refrigerate overnight.
2. Next day, add whipping cream and whip mixture until peaks are soft.
3. Spoon into dessert bowls or glasses. Refrigerate until ready to serve. Add a thin lemon slice for decoration and a few lemon wafers as an accompaniment.

THE PROOF OF the pudding is in the eating.

Henry Glapthorne, *The Hollander*, 1635

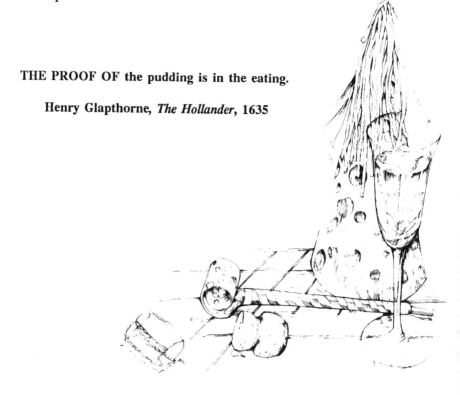

LEMON WAFERS

Makes 24 wafers

A perfect accompaniment to the Lemon Syllabub. These Lemon Wafers almost melt in your mouth.

4 tbsp	lemon rind, finely grated	60 ml
1/2 c	butter	125 ml
1/2 c	sugar	125 ml
1 tbsp	flour	15 ml
2 tbsp	milk	30 ml

1. In a small saucepan, combine all the ingredients. Stir at low heat until the butter melts.
2. On a well greased and floured cookie sheet, drop 4 or 5 spoonfuls at a time.
3. Bake in a preheated oven at 375°F (190°C) for 4 to 6 minutes until lightly browned. Let cool for 1 minute.
4. Then quickly wrap wafer around a wooden spoon handle. If wafer is too crispy to roll, put back in oven for 1 minute.
5. Slide wafer off handle. Cool. Serve.

CHOCOLATE TRUFFLES

Makes 24 truffles

Decadent. Chocolate Truffles are truly the perfect ending to dinner. Their simplicity belies the number of calories they have. But they are well worth all the extra calories.

6 oz	dark semi-sweet chocolate	200 g
4 tbsp	butter	60 ml
2 tsp	whipping cream	10 ml
1/4 c	unsweetened powdered cocoa	60 ml

1. In a small, heavy saucepan, at low heat, combine chocolate and butter until just melted. Add whipping cream.
2. Whisk well until mixture is smooth.
3. Pour into a bowl. Refrigerate for 30 minutes. Mixture should be firm.
4. Using a spoon, roll chocolate mixture into 1 inch (2.5 cm) sized balls. Makes 24 balls.
5. Roll chocolate balls in unsweetened powdered cocoa. Store in refrigerator covered. Remove 30 minutes before serving.

BRING ON THE dessert. I think I am about to die.

Pierette Brillat-Savarin, *soon to be famous last words,* 1911

PIRATE'S NIGHT RUM TODDY

Makes 1 serving

On a cold Nova Scotia night, nothing warms you up like a nice rum toddy. It reminds me of stories about pirates and buried treasure on Oak Island on the South Shore. Of course, our children get mugs of steaming cocoa to go with the stories.

2 oz	light or dark rum	60 ml
2 tbsp	sugar	30 ml
2	whole cloves	2
1	lemon slice	1
1 c	water	250 ml

1. Place a metal spoon in a heavy glass or heat-proof mug to prevent cracking.
2. Add rum, sugar, cloves, and lemon slice.
3. Pour boiling water in glass or mug. Stir well and serve.

And so to bed, to sleep off all the nonsense I just said.

Samuel Pepys

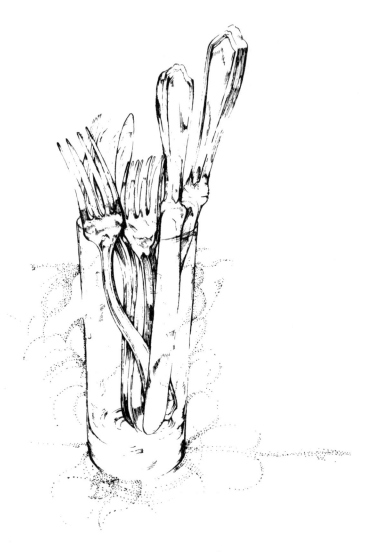

INDEX